AF730416

Secure One Per Page

NOTARY PUBLIC

& Signing Agent Journal

This journal belongs to :

Notary Public Logbook Entry #1

Date & Time: ___/___/___ ___:___ am/pm

Place:

Fee: $ __________

Travel: __________

Service

☐ Jurat ☐ Acknowledgement

☐ Certification ☐ Oath/Affirmation

☐ Others ______________________

Document Type: ______________________

Driver's License : _____ /_____ /_____

☐ Individual

☐ Credible Witness

Thumb Print:

☐ Driver's License

☐ Passport

☐ Known Personally

☐ ID Card

☐ Other __________

ID#: __________

Issued By: __________

Issued On: __/__/__

Expired On: __/__/__

Individual

Name:
(print)

Address:

Phone:
(or email)

Signature:

Witness

Name:
(print)

Address:

Phone:
(or email)

Signature:

Notes

Notary Public Logbook Entry #2

Date & Time: __/__/__ __:__ am/pm

Place:

Fee: $ __________

Travel: __________

Service

- [ ] Jurat
- [ ] Acknowledgement
- [ ] Certification
- [ ] Oath/Affirmation
- [ ] Others ____________________

Document Type: ____________________

Driver's License : _____ /_____ /_____

- [ ] Individual
- [ ] Credible Witness

Thumb Print:

- [ ] Driver's License
- [ ] Passport
- [ ] Known Personally
- [ ] ID Card
- [ ] Other __________

ID#: __________

Issued By: __________

Issued On: __/__/__

Expired On: __/__/__

Individual

Name:
(print)

Address:

Phone:
(or email)

Signature:

Witness

Name:
(print)

Address:

Phone:
(or email)

Signature:

Notes

Notary Public Logbook Entry #3

Date & Time: __/__/__ __:__ am/pm

Place:

Fee: $ ________

Travel: ________

Service

- [ ] Jurat
- [ ] Acknowledgement
- [ ] Certification
- [ ] Oath/Affirmation
- [ ] Others ____________________

Document Type: ____________________

Driver's License : _____ /_____ /_____

- [ ] Individual
- [ ] Credible Witness

Thumb Print:

- [ ] Driver's License
- [ ] Passport
- [ ] Known Personally
- [ ] ID Card
- [ ] Other ________

ID#: ________

Issued By: ________

Issued On: __/__/__

Expired On: __/__/__

Individual

Name:
(print)

Address:

Phone:
(or email)

Signature:

Witness

Name:
(print)

Address:

Phone:
(or email)

Signature:

Notes

Notary Public Logbook Entry #4

Date & Time: __/__/__ __:__ am/pm

Place:

Fee: $ ________

Travel: ________

Service

☐ Jurat ☐ Acknowledgement

☐ Certification ☐ Oath/Affirmation

☐ Others ____________

Document Type: ____________

Driver's License : ____ /____ /____

☐ Individual

☐ Credible Witness

Thumb Print:

☐ Driver's License

☐ Passport

☐ Known Personally

☐ ID Card

☐ Other ________

ID#: ________

Issued By: ________

Issued On: __/__/__

Expired On: __/__/__

Individual

Name:
(print)

Address:

Phone:
(or email)

Signature:

Witness

Name:
(print)

Address:

Phone:
(or email)

Signature:

Notes

Notary Public Logbook Entry #5

Date & Time: ___/___/___ ___:___ am/pm

Place:

Fee: $ ________

Travel: ________

Service

☐ Jurat ☐ Acknowledgement

☐ Certification ☐ Oath/Affirmation

☐ Others ____________________

Document Type: ____________________

Driver's License : _____ /_____ /_____

☐ Individual

☐ Credible Witness

Thumb Print:

☐ Driver's License

☐ Passport

☐ Known Personally

☐ ID Card

☐ Other ________

ID#: ________

Issued By: ________

Issued On: __/__/__

Expired On: __/__/__

Individual

Name:
(print)

Address:

Phone:
(or email)

Signature:

Witness

Name:
(print)

Address:

Phone:
(or email)

Signature:

Notes

Notary Public Logbook Entry #6

Date & Time: __/__/__ __:__ am/pm

Place:

Fee: $ ________

Travel: ________

Service

- [ ] Jurat
- [ ] Acknowledgement
- [ ] Certification
- [ ] Oath/Affirmation
- [ ] Others ____________

Document Type: ____________

Driver's License : _____ /_____ /_____

- [ ] Individual
- [ ] Credible Witness

Thumb Print:

- [ ] Driver's License
- [ ] Passport
- [ ] Known Personally
- [ ] ID Card
- [ ] Other ________

ID#: ________

Issued By: ________

Issued On: __/__/__

Expired On: __/__/__

Individual

Name:
(print)

Address:

Phone:
(or email)

Signature:

Witness

Name:
(print)

Address:

Phone:
(or email)

Signature:

Notes

Notary Public Logbook Entry #7

Date & Time: __/__/__ __:__ am/pm

Place:

Fee: $ ____________

Travel: ____________

Service

☐ Jurat ☐ Acknowledgement

☐ Certification ☐ Oath/Affirmation

☐ Others ____________________

Document Type: ____________________

Driver's License : _____ /_____ /_____

☐ Individual

☐ Credible Witness

Thumb Print:

☐ Driver's License

☐ Passport

☐ Known Personally

☐ ID Card

☐ Other ____________

ID#: ____________

Issued By: ____________

Issued On: __/__/__

Expired On: __/__/__

Individual

Name:
(print)

Address:

Phone:
(or email)

Signature:

Witness

Name:
(print)

Address:

Phone:
(or email)

Signature:

Notes

Notary Public Logbook Entry #8

Date & Time: __/__/__ __:__ am/pm

Place:

Fee: $ ________

Travel: ________

Service

☐ Jurat ☐ Acknowledgement

☐ Certification ☐ Oath/Affirmation

☐ Others ____________

Document Type: ____________

Driver's License : _____ /_____ /_____

☐ Individual

☐ Credible Witness

Thumb Print:

☐ Driver's License

☐ Passport

☐ Known Personally

☐ ID Card

☐ Other ________

ID#: ________

Issued By: ________

Issued On: __/__/__

Expired On: __/__/__

Individual

Name:
(print)

Address:

Phone:
(or email)

Signature:

Witness

Name:
(print)

Address:

Phone:
(or email)

Signature:

Notes

Notary Public Logbook Entry #9

Date & Time: __/__/__ __:__ am/pm

Place:

Fee: $ ________

Travel: ________

Service

- [ ] Jurat
- [ ] Acknowledgement
- [ ] Certification
- [ ] Oath/Affirmation
- [ ] Others ________________

Document Type: ________________

Driver's License : _____ /_____ /_____

- [ ] Individual
- [ ] Credible Witness

Thumb Print:

- [ ] Driver's License
- [ ] Passport
- [ ] Known Personally
- [ ] ID Card
- [ ] Other ________

ID#: ________

Issued By: ________

Issued On: __/__/__

Expired On: __/__/__

Individual

Name:
(print)

Address:

Phone:
(or email)

Signature:

Witness

Name:
(print)

Address:

Phone:
(or email)

Signature:

Notes

Notary Public Logbook Entry #10

Date & Time: __/__/__ __:__ am/pm

Place:

Fee: $ ________

Travel: ________

Service

- [ ] Jurat
- [ ] Acknowledgement
- [ ] Certification
- [ ] Oath/Affirmation
- [ ] Others ________

Document Type: ________

Driver's License : _____ /_____ /_____

- [ ] Individual
- [ ] Credible Witness

Thumb Print:

- [ ] Driver's License
- [ ] Passport
- [ ] Known Personally
- [ ] ID Card
- [ ] Other ________

ID#: ________

Issued By: ________

Issued On: __/__/__

Expired On: __/__/__

Individual

Name:
(print)

Address:

Phone:
(or email)

Signature:

Witness

Name:
(print)

Address:

Phone:
(or email)

Signature:

Notes

Notary Public Logbook Entry #11

Date & Time: __/__/__ __:__ am/pm

Place:

Fee: $ ________

Travel: ________

Service

- [ ] Jurat
- [ ] Acknowledgement
- [ ] Certification
- [ ] Oath/Affirmation
- [ ] Others ________________

Document Type: ________________

Driver's License : _____ /_____ /_____

- [ ] Individual
- [ ] Credible Witness

Thumb Print:

- [ ] Driver's License
- [ ] Passport
- [ ] Known Personally
- [ ] ID Card
- [ ] Other ________

ID#: ________

Issued By: ________

Issued On: __/__/__

Expired On:__/__/__

Individual

Name:
(print)

Address:

Phone:
(or email)

Signature:

Witness

Name:
(print)

Address:

Phone:
(or email)

Signature:

Notes

Notary Public Logbook Entry #12

Date & Time: __/__/__ __:__ am/pm

Place:

Fee: $ ______

Travel: ______

Service

- [ ] Jurat
- [ ] Acknowledgement
- [ ] Certification
- [ ] Oath/Affirmation
- [ ] Others ______

Document Type: ______

Driver's License : ___ /___ /___

- [ ] Individual
- [ ] Credible Witness

Thumb Print:

- [ ] Driver's License
- [ ] Passport
- [ ] Known Personally
- [ ] ID Card
- [ ] Other ______

ID#: ______

Issued By: ______

Issued On: __/__/__

Expired On: __/__/__

Individual

Name:
(print)

Address:

Phone:
(or email)

Signature:

Witness

Name:
(print)

Address:

Phone:
(or email)

Signature:

Notes

Notary Public Logbook Entry #13

Date & Time: __/__/__ __:__ am/pm

Place:

Fee: $ __________

Travel: __________

Service

- [ ] Jurat
- [ ] Acknowledgement
- [ ] Certification
- [ ] Oath/Affirmation
- [ ] Others ____________________

Document Type: ____________________

Driver's License : _____ /_____ /_____

- [ ] Individual
- [ ] Credible Witness

Thumb Print:

- [ ] Driver's License
- [ ] Passport
- [ ] Known Personally
- [ ] ID Card
- [ ] Other __________

ID#: __________

Issued By: __________

Issued On: __/__/__

Expired On: __/__/__

Individual

Name:
(print)

Address:

Phone:
(or email)

Signature:

Witness

Name:
(print)

Address:

Phone:
(or email)

Signature:

Notes

Notary Public Logbook Entry #14

Date & Time: __/__/__ __:__ am/pm

Place:

Fee: $ ________

Travel: ________

Service

☐ Jurat ☐ Acknowledgement

☐ Certification ☐ Oath/Affirmation

☐ Others ____________

Document Type: ____________

Driver's License : ____ /____ /____

☐ Individual

☐ Credible Witness

Thumb Print:

☐ Driver's License

☐ Passport

☐ Known Personally

☐ ID Card

☐ Other ________

ID#: ________

Issued By: ________

Issued On: __/__/__

Expired On: __/__/__

Individual

Name:
(print)

Address:

Phone:
(or email)

Signature:

Witness

Name:
(print)

Address:

Phone:
(or email)

Signature:

Notes

Notary Public Logbook Entry #15

Date & Time: __/__/__ __:__ am/pm

Place:

Fee: $ ________

Travel: ________

Service

☐ Jurat ☐ Acknowledgement

☐ Certification ☐ Oath/Affirmation

☐ Others ________________

Document Type: ________________

Driver's License : _____ /_____ /_____

☐ Individual

☐ Credible Witness

Thumb Print:

☐ Driver's License

☐ Passport

☐ Known Personally

☐ ID Card

☐ Other ________

ID#: ________

Issued By: ________

Issued On: __/__/__

Expired On: __/__/__

Individual

Name:
(print)

Address:

Phone:
(or email)

Signature:

Witness

Name:
(print)

Address:

Phone:
(or email)

Signature:

Notes

Notary Public Logbook Entry #16

Date & Time: __/__/__ __:__ am/pm

Place:

Fee: $ ________

Travel: ________

Service

- [ ] Jurat
- [ ] Acknowledgement
- [ ] Certification
- [ ] Oath/Affirmation
- [ ] Others ________

Document Type: ________

Driver's License : ____ /____ /____

- [ ] Individual
- [ ] Credible Witness

Thumb Print:

- [ ] Driver's License
- [ ] Passport
- [ ] Known Personally
- [ ] ID Card
- [ ] Other ________

ID#: ________

Issued By: ________

Issued On: __/__/__

Expired On: __/__/__

Individual

Name:
(print)

Address:

Phone:
(or email)

Signature:

Witness

Name:
(print)

Address:

Phone:
(or email)

Signature:

Notes

Notary Public Logbook Entry #17

Date & Time: __/__/__ __:__ am/pm

Place:

Fee: $ ________

Travel: ________

Service

- [ ] Jurat
- [ ] Acknowledgement
- [ ] Certification
- [ ] Oath/Affirmation
- [ ] Others ________________

Document Type: ________________

Driver's License : _____ /_____ /_____

- [ ] Individual
- [ ] Credible Witness

Thumb Print:

- [ ] Driver's License
- [ ] Passport
- [ ] Known Personally
- [ ] ID Card
- [ ] Other ________

ID#: ________

Issued By: ________

Issued On: __/__/__

Expired On: __/__/__

Individual

Name:
(print)

Address:

Phone:
(or email)

Signature:

Witness

Name:
(print)

Address:

Phone:
(or email)

Signature:

Notes

Notary Public Logbook Entry #18

Date & Time: __/__/__ __:__ am/pm

Place:

Fee: $ ________

Travel: ________

Service

- [ ] Jurat
- [ ] Acknowledgement
- [ ] Certification
- [ ] Oath/Affirmation
- [ ] Others ________

Document Type: ________

Driver's License : ____ /____ /____

- [ ] Individual
- [ ] Credible Witness

- [ ] Driver's License
- [ ] Passport
- [ ] Known Personally
- [ ] ID Card
- [ ] Other ________

Thumb Print:

ID#: ________

Issued By: ________

Issued On: __/__/__

Expired On: __/__/__

Individual

Name:
(print)

Address:

Phone:
(or email)

Signature:

Witness

Name:
(print)

Address:

Phone:
(or email)

Signature:

Notes

Notary Public Logbook Entry #19

Date & Time: __/__/__ __:__ am/pm

Place:

Fee: $ ________

Travel: ________

Service

- [ ] Jurat
- [ ] Acknowledgement
- [ ] Certification
- [ ] Oath/Affirmation
- [ ] Others ________

Document Type: ________

Driver's License : _____ /_____ /_____

- [ ] Individual
- [ ] Credible Witness

Thumb Print:

- [ ] Driver's License
- [ ] Passport
- [ ] Known Personally
- [ ] ID Card
- [ ] Other ________

ID#: ________

Issued By: ________

Issued On: __/__/__

Expired On: __/__/__

Individual

Name:
(print)

Address:

Phone:
(or email)

Signature:

Witness

Name:
(print)

Address:

Phone:
(or email)

Signature:

Notes

Notary Public Logbook Entry #20

Date & Time: __/__/__ __:__ am/pm

Place:

Fee: $ ________

Travel: ________

Service

- [ ] Jurat
- [ ] Acknowledgement
- [ ] Certification
- [ ] Oath/Affirmation
- [ ] Others ________________

Document Type: ________________

Driver's License : _____ /_____ /_____

- [ ] Individual
- [ ] Credible Witness

Thumb Print:

- [ ] Driver's License
- [ ] Passport
- [ ] Known Personally
- [ ] ID Card
- [ ] Other ________

ID#: ________

Issued By: ________

Issued On: __/__/__

Expired On: __/__/__

Individual

Name:
(print)

Address:

Phone:
(or email)

Signature:

Witness

Name:
(print)

Address:

Phone:
(or email)

Signature:

Notes

Notary Public Logbook Entry #21

Date & Time: __/__/__ __:__ am/pm

Place:

Fee: $ ________

Travel: ________

Service

☐ Jurat ☐ Acknowledgement

☐ Certification ☐ Oath/Affirmation

☐ Others ____________

Document Type: ____________

Driver's License : _____ /_____ /_____

☐ Individual

☐ Credible Witness

Thumb Print:

☐ Driver's License

☐ Passport

☐ Known Personally

☐ ID Card

☐ Other ________

ID#: ________

Issued By: ________

Issued On: __/__/__

Expired On: __/__/__

Individual

Name:
(print)

Address:

Phone:
(or email)

Signature:

Witness

Name:
(print)

Address:

Phone:
(or email)

Signature:

Notes

Notary Public Logbook Entry #22

Date & Time: __/__/__ __:__ am/pm

Place:

Fee: $ ________

Travel: ________

Service

☐ Jurat ☐ Acknowledgement

☐ Certification ☐ Oath/Affirmation

☐ Others ____________________

Document Type: ____________________

Driver's License : _____ /_____ /_____

☐ Individual

☐ Credible Witness

Thumb Print:

☐ Driver's License

☐ Passport

☐ Known Personally

☐ ID Card

☐ Other ________

ID#: ________

Issued By: ________

Issued On: __/__/__

Expired On: __/__/__

Individual

Name:
(print)

Address:

Phone:
(or email)

Signature:

Witness

Name:
(print)

Address:

Phone:
(or email)

Signature:

Notes

Notary Public Logbook Entry #23

Date & Time: __/__/__ __:__ am/pm

Place:

Fee: $ ______

Travel: ______

Service

- [ ] Jurat
- [ ] Acknowledgement
- [ ] Certification
- [ ] Oath/Affirmation
- [ ] Others ______

Document Type: ______

Driver's License : _____ /_____ /_____

- [ ] Individual
- [ ] Credible Witness

Thumb Print:

- [ ] Driver's License
- [ ] Passport
- [ ] Known Personally
- [ ] ID Card
- [ ] Other ______

ID#: ______

Issued By: ______

Issued On: __/__/__

Expired On: __/__/__

Individual

Name:
(print)

Address:

Phone:
(or email)

Signature:

Witness

Name:
(print)

Address:

Phone:
(or email)

Signature:

Notes

Notary Public Logbook Entry #24

Date & Time: __/__/__ __:__ am/pm

Place:

Fee: $ ________

Travel: ________

Service

☐ Jurat ☐ Acknowledgement

☐ Certification ☐ Oath/Affirmation

☐ Others ____________

Document Type: ____________

Driver's License : ____ /____ /____

☐ Individual

☐ Credible Witness

Thumb Print:

☐ Driver's License

☐ Passport

☐ Known Personally

☐ ID Card

☐ Other ________

ID#: ________

Issued By: ________

Issued On: __/__/__

Expired On: __/__/__

Individual

Name:
(print)

Address:

Phone:
(or email)

Signature:

Witness

Name:
(print)

Address:

Phone:
(or email)

Signature:

Notes

Notary Public Logbook Entry #25

Date & Time: ___/___/___ ___:___ am/pm

Place:

Fee: $ ___________

Travel: ___________

Service

☐ Jurat ☐ Acknowledgement

☐ Certification ☐ Oath/Affirmation

☐ Others ______________________

Document Type: ______________________

Driver's License : ______ /______ /______

☐ Individual

☐ Credible Witness

Thumb Print:

☐ Driver's License

☐ Passport

☐ Known Personally

☐ ID Card

☐ Other ___________

ID#: ___________

Issued By: ___________

Issued On: __/__/__

Expired On: __/__/__

Individual

Name:
(print)

Address:

Phone:
(or email)

Signature:

Witness

Name:
(print)

Address:

Phone:
(or email)

Signature:

Notes

Notary Public Logbook Entry #26

Date & Time: __/__/__ __:__ am/pm

Place:

Fee: $ ________

Travel: ________

Service

- [ ] Jurat
- [ ] Acknowledgement
- [ ] Certification
- [ ] Oath/Affirmation
- [ ] Others ____________

Document Type: ____________

Driver's License : ____ /____ /____

- [ ] Individual
- [ ] Credible Witness

Thumb Print:

- [ ] Driver's License
- [ ] Passport
- [ ] Known Personally
- [ ] ID Card
- [ ] Other ________

ID#: ________

Issued By: ________

Issued On: __/__/__

Expired On: __/__/__

Individual

Name:
(print)

Address:

Phone:
(or email)

Signature:

Witness

Name:
(print)

Address:

Phone:
(or email)

Signature:

Notes

Notary Public Logbook Entry #27

Date & Time: ___/___/___ ___:___ am/pm

Place:

Fee: $ ___________

Travel: ___________

Service

☐ Jurat ☐ Acknowledgement

☐ Certification ☐ Oath/Affirmation

☐ Others ___________________________

Document Type: ___________________________

Driver's License : ______ /______ /______

☐ Individual

☐ Credible Witness

Thumb Print:

☐ Driver's License

☐ Passport

☐ Known Personally

☐ ID Card

☐ Other ___________

ID#: ___________

Issued By: ___________

Issued On: __/__/__

Expired On:__/__/__

Individual

Name:
(print)

Address:

Phone:
(or email)

Signature:

Witness

Name:
(print)

Address:

Phone:
(or email)

Signature:

Notes

Notary Public Logbook Entry #28

Date & Time: __/__/__ __:__ am/pm

Place:

Fee: $ ________

Travel: ________

Service

- [ ] Jurat
- [ ] Acknowledgement
- [ ] Certification
- [ ] Oath/Affirmation
- [ ] Others ____________

Document Type: ____________

Driver's License : ____ /____ /____

- [ ] Individual
- [ ] Credible Witness

Thumb Print:

- [ ] Driver's License
- [ ] Passport
- [ ] Known Personally
- [ ] ID Card
- [ ] Other ________

ID#: ________

Issued By: ________

Issued On: __/__/__

Expired On: __/__/__

Individual

Name:
(print)

Address:

Phone:
(or email)

Signature:

Witness

Name:
(print)

Address:

Phone:
(or email)

Signature:

Notes

Notary Public Logbook Entry #29

Date & Time: __/__/__ __:__ am/pm

Place:

Fee: $ ________

Travel: ________

Service

☐ Jurat ☐ Acknowledgement

☐ Certification ☐ Oath/Affirmation

☐ Others ________________

Document Type: ________________

Driver's License : _____ /_____ /_____

☐ Individual

☐ Credible Witness

Thumb Print:

☐ Driver's License

☐ Passport

☐ Known Personally

☐ ID Card

☐ Other ________

ID#: ________

Issued By: ________

Issued On: __/__/__

Expired On: __/__/__

Individual

Name:
(print)

Address:

Phone:
(or email)

Signature:

Witness

Name:
(print)

Address:

Phone:
(or email)

Signature:

Notes

Notary Public Logbook Entry #30

Date & Time: __/__/__ __:__ am/pm

Place:

Fee: $ ________

Travel: ________

Service

- [ ] Jurat
- [ ] Acknowledgement
- [ ] Certification
- [ ] Oath/Affirmation
- [ ] Others ________________

Document Type: ________________

Driver's License : _____ /_____ /_____

- [ ] Individual
- [ ] Credible Witness

Thumb Print:

- [ ] Driver's License
- [ ] Passport
- [ ] Known Personally
- [ ] ID Card
- [ ] Other ________

ID#: ________

Issued By: ________

Issued On: __/__/__

Expired On: __/__/__

Individual

Name:
(print)

Address:

Phone:
(or email)

Signature:

Witness

Name:
(print)

Address:

Phone:
(or email)

Signature:

Notes

Notary Public Logbook Entry #31

Date & Time: __/__/__ __:__ am/pm

Place:

Fee: $ ________

Travel: ________

Service

☐ Jurat ☐ Acknowledgement

☐ Certification ☐ Oath/Affirmation

☐ Others ____________

Document Type: ____________

Driver's License : ____ /____ /____

☐ Individual

☐ Credible Witness

Thumb Print:

☐ Driver's License

☐ Passport

☐ Known Personally

☐ ID Card

☐ Other ________

ID#: ________

Issued By: ________

Issued On: __/__/__

Expired On: __/__/__

Individual

Name:
(print)

Address:

Phone:
(or email)

Signature:

Witness

Name:
(print)

Address:

Phone:
(or email)

Signature:

Notes

Notary Public Logbook Entry #32

Date & Time: __/__/__ __:__ am/pm

Place:

Fee: $ ________

Travel: ________

Service

☐ Jurat ☐ Acknowledgement

☐ Certification ☐ Oath/Affirmation

☐ Others ____________

Document Type: ____________

Driver's License : ____ /____ /____

Individual

Name:
(print)

Address:

Phone:
(or email)

Signature:

☐ Individual

☐ Credible Witness

Thumb Print:

☐ Driver's License

☐ Passport

☐ Known Personally

☐ ID Card

☐ Other ________

ID#: ________

Issued By: ________

Issued On: __/__/__

Expired On: __/__/__

Witness

Name:
(print)

Address:

Phone:
(or email)

Signature:

Notes

Notary Public Logbook Entry #33	
Date & Time: __/__/__ __:__ am/pm	
Place:	Fee: $ ________ Travel: ________

Service	
☐ Jurat	☐ Acknowledgement
☐ Certification	☐ Oath/Affirmation
☐ Others ________________	
Document Type: ________________	
Driver's License : _____ /_____ /_____	

☐ Individual ☐ Credible Witness	☐ Driver's License ☐ Passport ☐ Known Personally ☐ ID Card ☐ Other ________
Thumb Print:	ID#: ________ Issued By: ________ Issued On: __/__/__ Expired On: __/__/__

Individual
Name: (print)
Address:
Phone: (or email)
Signature:

Witness
Name: (print)
Address:
Phone: (or email)
Signature:

Notes

Notary Public Logbook Entry #34

Date & Time: ___/___/___ ___:___ am/pm

Place:

Fee: $ ___________

Travel: ___________

Service

☐ Jurat ☐ Acknowledgement

☐ Certification ☐ Oath/Affirmation

☐ Others ___________________

Document Type: ___________________

Driver's License : _____ /_____ /_____

Individual

Name:
(print)

Address:

Phone:
(or email)

Signature:

☐ Individual

☐ Credible Witness

Thumb Print:

☐ Driver's License

☐ Passport

☐ Known Personally

☐ ID Card

☐ Other ___________

ID#: ___________

Issued By: ___________

Issued On: __/__/__

Expired On: __/__/__

Witness

Name:
(print)

Address:

Phone:
(or email)

Signature:

Notes

Notary Public Logbook Entry #35

Date & Time: __/__/__ __:__ am/pm

Place:

Fee: $ ________

Travel: ________

Service

☐ Jurat ☐ Acknowledgement

☐ Certification ☐ Oath/Affirmation

☐ Others ____________

Document Type: ____________

Driver's License : ____ /____ /____

☐ Individual

☐ Credible Witness

Thumb Print:

☐ Driver's License

☐ Passport

☐ Known Personally

☐ ID Card

☐ Other ________

ID#: ________

Issued By: ________

Issued On: __/__/__

Expired On: __/__/__

Individual

Name:
(print)

Address:

Phone:
(or email)

Signature:

Witness

Name:
(print)

Address:

Phone:
(or email)

Signature:

Notes

Notary Public Logbook Entry #36

Date & Time: __/__/__ __:__ am/pm

Place:

Fee: $ ________

Travel: ________

Service

- [ ] Jurat
- [ ] Acknowledgement
- [ ] Certification
- [ ] Oath/Affirmation
- [ ] Others ____________

Document Type: ____________

Driver's License : ____ /____ /____

- [ ] Individual
- [ ] Credible Witness

Thumb Print:

- [ ] Driver's License
- [ ] Passport
- [ ] Known Personally
- [ ] ID Card
- [ ] Other ________

ID#: ________

Issued By: ________

Issued On: __/__/__

Expired On: __/__/__

Individual

Name:
(print)

Address:

Phone:
(or email)

Signature:

Witness

Name:
(print)

Address:

Phone:
(or email)

Signature:

Notes

Notary Public Logbook Entry #37

Date & Time: __/__/__ __:__ am/pm

Place:

Fee: $ ________

Travel: ________

Service

☐ Jurat ☐ Acknowledgement

☐ Certification ☐ Oath/Affirmation

☐ Others ________

Document Type: ________

Driver's License : ____ /____ /____

☐ Individual

☐ Credible Witness

Thumb Print:

☐ Driver's License

☐ Passport

☐ Known Personally

☐ ID Card

☐ Other ________

ID#: ________

Issued By: ________

Issued On: __/__/__

Expired On: __/__/__

Individual

Name:
(print)

Address:

Phone:
(or email)

Signature:

Witness

Name:
(print)

Address:

Phone:
(or email)

Signature:

Notes

Notary Public Logbook Entry #38

Date & Time: __/__/__ __:__ am/pm

Place:

Fee: $ ________

Travel: ________

Service

- ☐ Jurat
- ☐ Acknowledgement
- ☐ Certification
- ☐ Oath/Affirmation
- ☐ Others ________

Document Type: ________

Driver's License : ____ /____ /____

- ☐ Individual
- ☐ Credible Witness

Thumb Print:

- ☐ Driver's License
- ☐ Passport
- ☐ Known Personally
- ☐ ID Card
- ☐ Other ________

ID#: ________

Issued By: ________

Issued On: __/__/__

Expired On: __/__/__

Individual

Name:
(print)

Address:

Phone:
(or email)

Signature:

Witness

Name:
(print)

Address:

Phone:
(or email)

Signature:

Notes

Notary Public Logbook Entry #39

Date & Time: __/__/__ __:__ am/pm

Place:

Fee: $ __________

Travel: __________

Service

- [ ] Jurat
- [ ] Acknowledgement
- [ ] Certification
- [ ] Oath/Affirmation
- [ ] Others ____________________

Document Type: ____________________

Driver's License : _____ /_____ /_____

- [ ] Individual
- [ ] Credible Witness

Thumb Print:

- [ ] Driver's License
- [ ] Passport
- [ ] Known Personally
- [ ] ID Card
- [ ] Other __________

ID#: __________

Issued By: __________

Issued On: __/__/__

Expired On: __/__/__

Individual

Name:
(print)

Address:

Phone:
(or email)

Signature:

Witness

Name:
(print)

Address:

Phone:
(or email)

Signature:

Notes

Notary Public Logbook Entry #40

Date & Time: __/__/__ __:__ am/pm

Place:

Fee: $ ________

Travel: ________

Service

- [ ] Jurat
- [ ] Acknowledgement
- [ ] Certification
- [ ] Oath/Affirmation
- [ ] Others ________________

Document Type: ________________

Driver's License : _____ /_____ /_____

- [ ] Individual
- [ ] Credible Witness

Thumb Print:

- [ ] Driver's License
- [ ] Passport
- [ ] Known Personally
- [ ] ID Card
- [ ] Other ________

ID#: ________

Issued By: ________

Issued On: __/__/__

Expired On: __/__/__

Individual

Name:
(print)

Address:

Phone:
(or email)

Signature:

Witness

Name:
(print)

Address:

Phone:
(or email)

Signature:

Notes

Notary Public Logbook Entry #41

Date & Time: __/__/__ __:__ am/pm

Place:

Fee: $ ________

Travel: ________

Service

- [ ] Jurat
- [ ] Acknowledgement
- [ ] Certification
- [ ] Oath/Affirmation
- [ ] Others ____________

Document Type: ____________

Driver's License : _____ /_____ /_____

- [ ] Individual
- [ ] Credible Witness

Thumb Print:

- [ ] Driver's License
- [ ] Passport
- [ ] Known Personally
- [ ] ID Card
- [ ] Other ________

ID#: ________

Issued By: ________

Issued On: __/__/__

Expired On: __/__/__

Individual

Name:
(print)

Address:

Phone:
(or email)

Signature:

Witness

Name:
(print)

Address:

Phone:
(or email)

Signature:

Notes

Notary Public Logbook Entry #42

Date & Time: __/__/__ __:__ am/pm

Place:

Fee: $ ______

Travel: ______

Service

- [ ] Jurat
- [ ] Acknowledgement
- [ ] Certification
- [ ] Oath/Affirmation
- [ ] Others ______

Document Type: ______

Driver's License : ___ /___ /___

- [ ] Individual
- [ ] Credible Witness

Thumb Print:

- [ ] Driver's License
- [ ] Passport
- [ ] Known Personally
- [ ] ID Card
- [ ] Other ______

ID#: ______

Issued By: ______

Issued On: __/__/__

Expired On: __/__/__

Individual

Name:
(print)

Address:

Phone:
(or email)

Signature:

Witness

Name:
(print)

Address:

Phone:
(or email)

Signature:

Notes

Notary Public Logbook Entry #43

Date & Time: __/__/__ __:__ am/pm

Place:

Fee: $ ________

Travel: ________

Service

- [ ] Jurat
- [ ] Acknowledgement
- [ ] Certification
- [ ] Oath/Affirmation
- [ ] Others ________________

Document Type: ________________

Driver's License : _____ /_____ /_____

- [ ] Individual
- [ ] Credible Witness

Thumb Print:

- [ ] Driver's License
- [ ] Passport
- [ ] Known Personally
- [ ] ID Card
- [ ] Other ________

ID#: ________

Issued By: ________

Issued On: __/__/__

Expired On: __/__/__

Individual

Name:
(print)

Address:

Phone:
(or email)

Signature:

Witness

Name:
(print)

Address:

Phone:
(or email)

Signature:

Notes

Notary Public Logbook Entry #44

Date & Time: __/__/__ __:__ am/pm

Place:

Fee: $ ________

Travel: ________

Service

☐ Jurat ☐ Acknowledgement

☐ Certification ☐ Oath/Affirmation

☐ Others ________________

Document Type: ________________

Driver's License : _____ /_____ /_____

☐ Individual

☐ Credible Witness

Thumb Print:

☐ Driver's License

☐ Passport

☐ Known Personally

☐ ID Card

☐ Other ________

ID#: ________

Issued By: ________

Issued On: __/__/__

Expired On: __/__/__

Individual

Name:
(print)

Address:

Phone:
(or email)

Signature:

Witness

Name:
(print)

Address:

Phone:
(or email)

Signature:

Notes

Notary Public Logbook Entry #45

Date & Time: __/__/__ __:__ am/pm

Place:

Fee: $ __________

Travel: __________

Service

- [ ] Jurat
- [ ] Acknowledgement
- [ ] Certification
- [ ] Oath/Affirmation
- [ ] Others __________________

Document Type: __________________

Driver's License : _____ /_____ /_____

- [ ] Individual
- [ ] Credible Witness

Thumb Print:

- [ ] Driver's License
- [ ] Passport
- [ ] Known Personally
- [ ] ID Card
- [ ] Other __________

ID#: __________

Issued By: __________

Issued On: __/__/__

Expired On: __/__/__

Individual

Name:
(print)

Address:

Phone:
(or email)

Signature:

Witness

Name:
(print)

Address:

Phone:
(or email)

Signature:

Notes

Notary Public Logbook Entry #46

Date & Time: __/__/__ __:__ am/pm

Place:

Fee: $ ________

Travel: ________

Service

☐ Jurat ☐ Acknowledgement

☐ Certification ☐ Oath/Affirmation

☐ Others ____________

Document Type: ____________

Driver's License : ____ /____ /____

☐ Individual

☐ Credible Witness

Thumb Print:

☐ Driver's License

☐ Passport

☐ Known Personally

☐ ID Card

☐ Other ________

ID#: ________

Issued By: ________

Issued On: __/__/__

Expired On: __/__/__

Individual

Name:
(print)

Address:

Phone:
(or email)

Signature:

Witness

Name:
(print)

Address:

Phone:
(or email)

Signature:

Notes

Notary Public Logbook Entry #47

Date & Time: __/__/__ __:__ am/pm

Place:

Fee: $ ______

Travel: ______

Service

- [ ] Jurat
- [ ] Acknowledgement
- [ ] Certification
- [ ] Oath/Affirmation
- [ ] Others ______

Document Type: ______

Driver's License : ____ /____ /____

- [ ] Individual
- [ ] Credible Witness

Thumb Print:

- [ ] Driver's License
- [ ] Passport
- [ ] Known Personally
- [ ] ID Card
- [ ] Other ______

ID#: ______

Issued By: ______

Issued On: __/__/__

Expired On: __/__/__

Individual

Name:
(print)

Address:

Phone:
(or email)

Signature:

Witness

Name:
(print)

Address:

Phone:
(or email)

Signature:

Notes

Notary Public Logbook Entry #48	
Date & Time: __/__/__ __:__ am/pm	
Place:	Fee: $ ______ Travel: ______

Service	
☐ Jurat	☐ Acknowledgement
☐ Certification	☐ Oath/Affirmation
☐ Others	__________

Document Type: __________

Driver's License : ____ /____ /____

Individual
Name: (print)
Address:
Phone: (or email)
Signature:

☐ Individual ☐ Credible Witness	☐ Driver's License ☐ Passport ☐ Known Personally ☐ ID Card ☐ Other ______
Thumb Print:	ID#: ______ Issued By: ______ Issued On: __/__/__ Expired On: __/__/__

Witness
Name: (print)
Address:
Phone: (or email)
Signature:

Notes

Notary Public Logbook Entry #49

Date & Time: __/__/__ __:__ am/pm

Place:

Fee: $ ________

Travel: ________

Service

- [ ] Jurat
- [ ] Acknowledgement
- [ ] Certification
- [ ] Oath/Affirmation
- [ ] Others ________________

Document Type: ________________

Driver's License : _____ /_____ /_____

- [ ] Individual
- [ ] Credible Witness

Thumb Print:

- [ ] Driver's License
- [ ] Passport
- [ ] Known Personally
- [ ] ID Card
- [ ] Other ________

ID#: ________

Issued By: ________

Issued On: __/__/__

Expired On: __/__/__

Individual

Name:
(print)

Address:

Phone:
(or email)

Signature:

Witness

Name:
(print)

Address:

Phone:
(or email)

Signature:

Notes

Notary Public Logbook Entry #50

Date & Time: __/__/__ __:__ am/pm

Place:

Fee: $ ________

Travel: ________

Service

- [ ] Jurat
- [ ] Acknowledgement
- [ ] Certification
- [ ] Oath/Affirmation
- [ ] Others ____________

Document Type: ____________

Driver's License : ____ /____ /____

- [ ] Individual
- [ ] Credible Witness

Thumb Print:

- [ ] Driver's License
- [ ] Passport
- [ ] Known Personally
- [ ] ID Card
- [ ] Other ________

ID#: ________

Issued By: ________

Issued On: __/__/__

Expired On: __/__/__

Individual

Name:
(print)

Address:

Phone:
(or email)

Signature:

Witness

Name:
(print)

Address:

Phone:
(or email)

Signature:

Notes

Notary Public Logbook Entry #51

Date & Time: __/__/__ __:__ am/pm

Place:

Fee: $ ________

Travel: ________

Service

☐ Jurat ☐ Acknowledgement

☐ Certification ☐ Oath/Affirmation

☐ Others ________

Document Type: ________

Driver's License : ____ /____ /____

☐ Individual

☐ Credible Witness

Thumb Print:

☐ Driver's License

☐ Passport

☐ Known Personally

☐ ID Card

☐ Other ________

ID#: ________

Issued By: ________

Issued On: __/__/__

Expired On: __/__/__

Individual

Name:
(print)

Address:

Phone:
(or email)

Signature:

Witness

Name:
(print)

Address:

Phone:
(or email)

Signature:

Notes

Notary Public Logbook Entry #52

Date & Time: __/__/__ __:__ am/pm

Place:

Fee: $ ________

Travel: ________

Service

- [ ] Jurat
- [ ] Acknowledgement
- [ ] Certification
- [ ] Oath/Affirmation
- [ ] Others ____________

Document Type: ____________

Driver's License : ____ /____ /____

- [ ] Individual
- [ ] Credible Witness

Thumb Print:

- [ ] Driver's License
- [ ] Passport
- [ ] Known Personally
- [ ] ID Card
- [ ] Other ________

ID#: ________

Issued By: ________

Issued On: __/__/__

Expired On: __/__/__

Individual

Name:
(print)

Address:

Phone:
(or email)

Signature:

Witness

Name:
(print)

Address:

Phone:
(or email)

Signature:

Notes

Notary Public Logbook Entry #53

Date & Time: ___/___/___ ___:___ am/pm

Place:

Fee: $ ___________

Travel: ___________

Service

- [ ] Jurat
- [ ] Acknowledgement
- [ ] Certification
- [ ] Oath/Affirmation
- [ ] Others ____________________

Document Type: ____________________

Driver's License : _____ /_____ /_____

- [ ] Individual
- [ ] Credible Witness

Thumb Print:

- [ ] Driver's License
- [ ] Passport
- [ ] Known Personally
- [ ] ID Card
- [ ] Other ___________

ID#: ___________

Issued By: ___________

Issued On: __/__/__

Expired On: __/__/__

Individual

Name:
(print)

Address:

Phone:
(or email)

Signature:

Witness

Name:
(print)

Address:

Phone:
(or email)

Signature:

Notes

Notary Public Logbook Entry #54

Date & Time: ___/___/___ ___:___ am/pm

Place:

Fee: $ ___________

Travel: ___________

Service

☐ Jurat ☐ Acknowledgement

☐ Certification ☐ Oath/Affirmation

☐ Others ___________________________

Document Type: ___________________________

Driver's License : _____ /_____ /_____

☐ Individual

☐ Credible Witness

Thumb Print:

☐ Driver's License

☐ Passport

☐ Known Personally

☐ ID Card

☐ Other ___________

ID#: ___________

Issued By: ___________

Issued On: __/__/__

Expired On: __/__/__

Individual

Name:
(print)

Address:

Phone:
(or email)

Signature:

Witness

Name:
(print)

Address:

Phone:
(or email)

Signature:

Notes

Notary Public Logbook Entry #55

Date & Time: __/__/__ __:__ am/pm

Place:

Fee: $ ________

Travel: ________

Service

☐ Jurat ☐ Acknowledgement

☐ Certification ☐ Oath/Affirmation

☐ Others ________

Document Type: ________

Driver's License : ____ /____ /____

☐ Individual

☐ Credible Witness

Thumb Print:

☐ Driver's License

☐ Passport

☐ Known Personally

☐ ID Card

☐ Other ________

ID#: ________

Issued By: ________

Issued On: __/__/__

Expired On: __/__/__

Individual

Name:
(print)

Address:

Phone:
(or email)

Signature:

Witness

Name:
(print)

Address:

Phone:
(or email)

Signature:

Notes

Notary Public Logbook Entry #56

Date & Time: __/__/__ __:__ am/pm

Place:

Fee: $ __________

Travel: __________

Service

- [ ] Jurat
- [ ] Acknowledgement
- [ ] Certification
- [ ] Oath/Affirmation
- [ ] Others ____________________

Document Type: ____________________

Driver's License : _____ /_____ /_____

- [ ] Individual
- [ ] Credible Witness

Thumb Print:

- [ ] Driver's License
- [ ] Passport
- [ ] Known Personally
- [ ] ID Card
- [ ] Other __________

ID#: __________

Issued By: __________

Issued On: __/__/__

Expired On: __/__/__

Individual

Name:
(print)

Address:

Phone:
(or email)

Signature:

Witness

Name:
(print)

Address:

Phone:
(or email)

Signature:

Notes

Notary Public Logbook Entry #57

Date & Time: ___/___/___ ___:___ am/pm

Place:

Fee: $ ___________

Travel: ___________

Service

☐ Jurat ☐ Acknowledgement

☐ Certification ☐ Oath/Affirmation

☐ Others ________________________

Document Type: ________________________

Driver's License : ______ /______ /______

☐ Individual

☐ Credible Witness

Thumb Print:

☐ Driver's License

☐ Passport

☐ Known Personally

☐ ID Card

☐ Other ___________

ID#: __________

Issued By: __________

Issued On: __/__/__

Expired On: __/__/__

Individual

Name:
(print)

Address:

Phone:
(or email)

Signature:

Witness

Name:
(print)

Address:

Phone:
(or email)

Signature:

Notes

Notary Public Logbook Entry #58

Date & Time: __/__/__ __:__ am/pm

Place:

Fee: $ __________

Travel: __________

Service

- [ ] Jurat
- [ ] Acknowledgement
- [ ] Certification
- [ ] Oath/Affirmation
- [ ] Others ____________________

Document Type: ____________________

Driver's License : _____ /_____ /_____

- [ ] Individual
- [ ] Credible Witness

Thumb Print:

- [ ] Driver's License
- [ ] Passport
- [ ] Known Personally
- [ ] ID Card
- [ ] Other __________

ID#: __________

Issued By: __________

Issued On: __/__/__

Expired On: __/__/__

Individual

Name:
(print)

Address:

Phone:
(or email)

Signature:

Witness

Name:
(print)

Address:

Phone:
(or email)

Signature:

Notes

Notary Public Logbook Entry #59

Date & Time: __/__/__ __:__ am/pm

Place:

Fee: $ ________

Travel: ________

Service

☐ Jurat ☐ Acknowledgement

☐ Certification ☐ Oath/Affirmation

☐ Others ____________

Document Type: ____________

Driver's License : ____ /____ /____

☐ Individual

☐ Credible Witness

Thumb Print:

☐ Driver's License

☐ Passport

☐ Known Personally

☐ ID Card

☐ Other ________

ID#: ________

Issued By: ________

Issued On: __/__/__

Expired On: __/__/__

Individual

Name:
(print)

Address:

Phone:
(or email)

Signature:

Witness

Name:
(print)

Address:

Phone:
(or email)

Signature:

Notes

Notary Public Logbook Entry #60

Date & Time: __/__/__ __:__ am/pm

Place:

Fee: $ ______

Travel: ______

Service

- [ ] Jurat
- [ ] Acknowledgement
- [ ] Certification
- [ ] Oath/Affirmation
- [ ] Others ______

Document Type: ______

Driver's License : ____ /____ /____

- [ ] Individual
- [ ] Credible Witness

Thumb Print:

- [ ] Driver's License
- [ ] Passport
- [ ] Known Personally
- [ ] ID Card
- [ ] Other ______

ID#: ______

Issued By: ______

Issued On: __/__/__

Expired On: __/__/__

Individual

Name:
(print)

Address:

Phone:
(or email)

Signature:

Witness

Name:
(print)

Address:

Phone:
(or email)

Signature:

Notes

Notary Public Logbook Entry #61

Date & Time: __/__/__ __:__ am/pm

Place:

Fee: $ ________

Travel: ________

Service

- [ ] Jurat
- [ ] Acknowledgement
- [ ] Certification
- [ ] Oath/Affirmation
- [ ] Others ____________

Document Type: ____________

Driver's License : ____ /____ /____

Individual

Name: (print)

Address:

Phone: (or email)

Signature:

- [ ] Individual
- [ ] Credible Witness

Thumb Print:

- [ ] Driver's License
- [ ] Passport
- [ ] Known Personally
- [ ] ID Card
- [ ] Other ________

ID#: ________

Issued By: ________

Issued On: __/__/__

Expired On: __/__/__

Witness

Name: (print)

Address:

Phone: (or email)

Signature:

Notes

Notary Public Logbook Entry #62

Date & Time: ___/___/___ ___:___ am/pm

Place:

Fee: $ ___________

Travel: ___________

Service

☐ Jurat ☐ Acknowledgement

☐ Certification ☐ Oath/Affirmation

☐ Others ____________________

Document Type: ____________________

Driver's License : _____ /_____ /_____

☐ Individual

☐ Credible Witness

Thumb Print:

☐ Driver's License

☐ Passport

☐ Known Personally

☐ ID Card

☐ Other __________

ID#: __________

Issued By: __________

Issued On: __/__/__

Expired On:__/__/__

Individual

Name:
(print)

Address:

Phone:
(or email)

Signature:

Witness

Name:
(print)

Address:

Phone:
(or email)

Signature:

Notes

Notary Public Logbook Entry #63

Date & Time: ___/___/___ ___:___ am/pm

Place:

Fee: $ ___________

Travel: ___________

Service

☐ Jurat ☐ Acknowledgement

☐ Certification ☐ Oath/Affirmation

☐ Others ___________________________

Document Type: ___________________________

Driver's License : _____ /_____ /_____

☐ Individual

☐ Credible Witness

Thumb Print:

☐ Driver's License

☐ Passport

☐ Known Personally

☐ ID Card

☐ Other ___________

ID#: ___________

Issued By: ___________

Issued On: __/__/__

Expired On: __/__/__

Individual

Name:
(print)

Address:

Phone:
(or email)

Signature:

Witness

Name:
(print)

Address:

Phone:
(or email)

Signature:

Notes

Notary Public Logbook Entry #64

Date & Time: __/__/__ __:__ am/pm

Place:

Fee: $ ________

Travel: ________

Service

- [ ] Jurat
- [ ] Acknowledgement
- [ ] Certification
- [ ] Oath/Affirmation
- [ ] Others ________

Document Type: ________

Driver's License : ____ /____ /____

- [ ] Individual
- [ ] Credible Witness

Thumb Print:

- [ ] Driver's License
- [ ] Passport
- [ ] Known Personally
- [ ] ID Card
- [ ] Other ________

ID#: ________

Issued By: ________

Issued On: __/__/__

Expired On: __/__/__

Individual

Name:
(print)

Address:

Phone:
(or email)

Signature:

Witness

Name:
(print)

Address:

Phone:
(or email)

Signature:

Notes

Notary Public Logbook Entry #65	
Date & Time: __/__/__ __:__ am/pm	
Place:	Fee: $ ________ Travel: ________

Service	
☐ Jurat	☐ Acknowledgement
☐ Certification	☐ Oath/Affirmation
☐ Others ____________	

Document Type: ____________

Driver's License : ____ /____ /____

Individual
Name: (print)
Address:
Phone: (or email)
Signature:

☐ Individual ☐ Credible Witness	☐ Driver's License ☐ Passport ☐ Known Personally ☐ ID Card ☐ Other ________
Thumb Print:	ID#: ________ Issued By: ________ Issued On: __/__/__ Expired On: __/__/__

Witness
Name: (print)
Address:
Phone: (or email)
Signature:

Notes

Notary Public Logbook Entry #66

Date & Time: ___/___/___ ___:___ am/pm

Place:

Fee: $ ___________

Travel: ___________

Service

☐ Jurat ☐ Acknowledgement

☐ Certification ☐ Oath/Affirmation

☐ Others ___________________________

Document Type: ___________________________

Driver's License : ______ /______ /______

☐ Individual

☐ Credible Witness

Thumb Print:

☐ Driver's License

☐ Passport

☐ Known Personally

☐ ID Card

☐ Other ___________

ID#: ___________

Issued By: ___________

Issued On: __/__/__

Expired On: __/__/__

Individual

Name:
(print)

Address:

Phone:
(or email)

Signature:

Witness

Name:
(print)

Address:

Phone:
(or email)

Signature:

Notes

Notary Public Logbook Entry #67

Date & Time: __/__/__ __:__ am/pm

Place:

Fee: $ __________

Travel: __________

Service

- [ ] Jurat
- [ ] Acknowledgement
- [ ] Certification
- [ ] Oath/Affirmation
- [ ] Others ____________________

Document Type: ____________________

Driver's License : _____ /_____ /_____

- [ ] Individual
- [ ] Credible Witness

Thumb Print:

- [ ] Driver's License
- [ ] Passport
- [ ] Known Personally
- [ ] ID Card
- [ ] Other __________

ID#: __________

Issued By: __________

Issued On: __/__/__

Expired On: __/__/__

Individual

Name:
(print)

Address:

Phone:
(or email)

Signature:

Witness

Name:
(print)

Address:

Phone:
(or email)

Signature:

Notes

Notary Public Logbook Entry #68

Date & Time: __/__/__ __:__ am/pm

Place:

Fee: $ ________

Travel: ________

Service

☐ Jurat ☐ Acknowledgement

☐ Certification ☐ Oath/Affirmation

☐ Others ____________

Document Type: ____________

Driver's License : ____ /____ /____

☐ Individual

☐ Credible Witness

Thumb Print:

☐ Driver's License

☐ Passport

☐ Known Personally

☐ ID Card

☐ Other ________

ID#: ________

Issued By: ________

Issued On: __/__/__

Expired On: __/__/__

Individual

Name:
(print)

Address:

Phone:
(or email)

Signature:

Witness

Name:
(print)

Address:

Phone:
(or email)

Signature:

Notes

Notary Public Logbook Entry #69	
Date & Time: __/__/__ __:__ am/pm	
Place:	Fee: $ ______ Travel: ______

Service	
☐ Jurat	☐ Acknowledgement
☐ Certification	☐ Oath/Affirmation
☐ Others	________
Document Type: ________	
Driver's License : ____ /____ /____	

Individual
Name: (print)
Address:
Phone: (or email)
Signature:

☐ Individual ☐ Credible Witness	☐ Driver's License ☐ Passport ☐ Known Personally ☐ ID Card ☐ Other ______
Thumb Print:	ID#: ______ Issued By: ______ Issued On: __/__/__ Expired On: __/__/__

Witness
Name: (print)
Address:
Phone: (or email)
Signature:

Notes

Notary Public Logbook Entry #70

Date & Time: __/__/__ __:__ am/pm

Place:

Fee: $ ________

Travel: ________

Service

☐ Jurat ☐ Acknowledgement

☐ Certification ☐ Oath/Affirmation

☐ Others ____________

Document Type: ____________

Driver's License : ____ /____ /____

☐ Individual

☐ Credible Witness

Thumb Print:

☐ Driver's License

☐ Passport

☐ Known Personally

☐ ID Card

☐ Other ________

ID#: ________

Issued By: ________

Issued On: __/__/__

Expired On: __/__/__

Individual

Name:
(print)

Address:

Phone:
(or email)

Signature:

Witness

Name:
(print)

Address:

Phone:
(or email)

Signature:

Notes

Notary Public Logbook Entry #71

Date & Time: __/__/__ __:__ am/pm

Place:

Fee: $ ________

Travel: ________

Service

☐ Jurat ☐ Acknowledgement

☐ Certification ☐ Oath/Affirmation

☐ Others ________________

Document Type: ________________

Driver's License : _____ /_____ /_____

☐ Individual

☐ Credible Witness

Thumb Print:

☐ Driver's License

☐ Passport

☐ Known Personally

☐ ID Card

☐ Other ________

ID#: ________

Issued By: ________

Issued On: __/__/__

Expired On: __/__/__

Individual

Name:
(print)

Address:

Phone:
(or email)

Signature:

Witness

Name:
(print)

Address:

Phone:
(or email)

Signature:

Notes

Notary Public Logbook Entry #72

Date & Time: __/__/__ __:__ am/pm

Place:

Fee: $ ________

Travel: ________

Service

- [ ] Jurat
- [ ] Acknowledgement
- [ ] Certification
- [ ] Oath/Affirmation
- [ ] Others ________________

Document Type: ________________

Driver's License : _____ /_____ /_____

- [ ] Individual
- [ ] Credible Witness

Thumb Print:

- [ ] Driver's License
- [ ] Passport
- [ ] Known Personally
- [ ] ID Card
- [ ] Other ________

ID#: ________

Issued By: ________

Issued On: __/__/__

Expired On: __/__/__

Individual

Name:
(print)

Address:

Phone:
(or email)

Signature:

Witness

Name:
(print)

Address:

Phone:
(or email)

Signature:

Notes

Notary Public Logbook Entry #73

Date & Time: __/__/__ __:__ am/pm

Place:

Fee: $ ________

Travel: ________

Service

☐ Jurat ☐ Acknowledgement

☐ Certification ☐ Oath/Affirmation

☐ Others ____________

Document Type: ____________

Driver's License : _____ /_____ /_____

☐ Individual

☐ Credible Witness

Thumb Print:

☐ Driver's License

☐ Passport

☐ Known Personally

☐ ID Card

☐ Other ________

ID#: ________

Issued By: ________

Issued On: __/__/__

Expired On: __/__/__

Individual

Name:
(print)

Address:

Phone:
(or email)

Signature:

Witness

Name:
(print)

Address:

Phone:
(or email)

Signature:

Notes

Notary Public Logbook Entry #74	
Date & Time: __/__/__ __:__ am/pm	
Place:	Fee: $ ______ Travel: ______

Service	
☐ Jurat	☐ Acknowledgement
☐ Certification	☐ Oath/Affirmation
☐ Others	__________

Document Type: __________

Driver's License : ____ /____ /____

☐ Individual ☐ Credible Witness	☐ Driver's License ☐ Passport ☐ Known Personally ☐ ID Card ☐ Other ______
Thumb Print:	ID#: ______ Issued By: ______ Issued On: __/__/__ Expired On: __/__/__

Individual
Name: (print)
Address:
Phone: (or email)
Signature:

Witness
Name: (print)
Address:
Phone: (or email)
Signature:

Notes

Notary Public Logbook Entry #75

Date & Time: __/__/__ __:__ am/pm

Place:

Fee: $ ______

Travel: ______

Service

☐ Jurat ☐ Acknowledgement

☐ Certification ☐ Oath/Affirmation

☐ Others ______

Document Type: ______

Driver's License : ____ /____ /____

☐ Individual

☐ Credible Witness

Thumb Print:

☐ Driver's License

☐ Passport

☐ Known Personally

☐ ID Card

☐ Other ______

ID#: ______

Issued By: ______

Issued On: __/__/__

Expired On: __/__/__

Individual

Name:
(print)

Address:

Phone:
(or email)

Signature:

Witness

Name:
(print)

Address:

Phone:
(or email)

Signature:

Notes

Notary Public Logbook Entry #76	
Date & Time: __/__/__ __:__ am/pm	
Place:	Fee: $ ______ Travel: ______

Service	
☐ Jurat	☐ Acknowledgement
☐ Certification	☐ Oath/Affirmation
☐ Others	__________

Document Type: __________

Driver's License : ____ /____ /____

☐ Individual ☐ Credible Witness	☐ Driver's License ☐ Passport ☐ Known Personally ☐ ID Card ☐ Other ______
Thumb Print:	ID#: ______ Issued By: ______ Issued On: __/__/__ Expired On: __/__/__

Individual
Name: (print)
Address:
Phone: (or email)
Signature:

Witness
Name: (print)
Address:
Phone: (or email)
Signature:

Notes

Notary Public Logbook Entry #77

Date & Time: __/__/__ __:__ am/pm

Place:

Fee: $ ________

Travel: ________

Service

☐ Jurat ☐ Acknowledgement

☐ Certification ☐ Oath/Affirmation

☐ Others ________________

Document Type: ________________

Driver's License : _____ /_____ /_____

☐ Individual

☐ Credible Witness

Thumb Print:

☐ Driver's License

☐ Passport

☐ Known Personally

☐ ID Card

☐ Other ________

ID#: ________

Issued By: ________

Issued On: __/__/__

Expired On: __/__/__

Individual

Name:
(print)

Address:

Phone:
(or email)

Signature:

Witness

Name:
(print)

Address:

Phone:
(or email)

Signature:

Notes

Notary Public Logbook Entry #78

Date & Time: __/__/__ __:__ am/pm

Place:

Fee: $ ________

Travel: ________

Service

☐ Jurat ☐ Acknowledgement

☐ Certification ☐ Oath/Affirmation

☐ Others ____________

Document Type: ____________

Driver's License : _____ /_____ /_____

☐ Individual

☐ Credible Witness

Thumb Print:

☐ Driver's License

☐ Passport

☐ Known Personally

☐ ID Card

☐ Other __________

ID#: __________

Issued By: __________

Issued On: __/__/__

Expired On: __/__/__

Individual

Name: (print)

Address:

Phone: (or email)

Signature:

Witness

Name: (print)

Address:

Phone: (or email)

Signature:

Notes

Notary Public Logbook Entry #79

Date & Time: __/__/__ __:__ am/pm

Place:

Fee: $ ________

Travel: ________

Service

- [ ] Jurat
- [ ] Acknowledgement
- [ ] Certification
- [ ] Oath/Affirmation
- [ ] Others ________________

Document Type: ________________

Driver's License : _____ /_____ /_____

- [ ] Individual
- [ ] Credible Witness

Thumb Print:

- [ ] Driver's License
- [ ] Passport
- [ ] Known Personally
- [ ] ID Card
- [ ] Other ________

ID#: ________

Issued By: ________

Issued On: __/__/__

Expired On: __/__/__

Individual

Name:
(print)

Address:

Phone:
(or email)

Signature:

Witness

Name:
(print)

Address:

Phone:
(or email)

Signature:

Notes

Notary Public Logbook Entry #80

Date & Time: __/__/__ __:__ am/pm

Place:

Fee: $ ________

Travel: ________

Service

- [ ] Jurat
- [ ] Acknowledgement
- [ ] Certification
- [ ] Oath/Affirmation
- [ ] Others ________________

Document Type: ________________

Driver's License : _____ /_____ /_____

- [ ] Individual
- [ ] Credible Witness

Thumb Print:

- [ ] Driver's License
- [ ] Passport
- [ ] Known Personally
- [ ] ID Card
- [ ] Other ________

ID#: ________

Issued By: ________

Issued On: __/__/__

Expired On: __/__/__

Individual

Name:
(print)

Address:

Phone:
(or email)

Signature:

Witness

Name:
(print)

Address:

Phone:
(or email)

Signature:

Notes

Notary Public Logbook Entry #81

Date & Time: __/__/__ __:__ am/pm

Place:

Fee: $ ________

Travel: ________

Service

- [ ] Jurat
- [ ] Acknowledgement
- [ ] Certification
- [ ] Oath/Affirmation
- [ ] Others ________________

Document Type: ________________

Driver's License : _____ /_____ /_____

- [ ] Individual
- [ ] Credible Witness

Thumb Print:

- [ ] Driver's License
- [ ] Passport
- [ ] Known Personally
- [ ] ID Card
- [ ] Other ________

ID#: ________

Issued By: ________

Issued On: __/__/__

Expired On: __/__/__

Individual

Name:
(print)

Address:

Phone:
(or email)

Signature:

Witness

Name:
(print)

Address:

Phone:
(or email)

Signature:

Notes

Notary Public Logbook Entry #82

Date & Time: __/__/__ __:__ am/pm

Place:

Fee: $ ________

Travel: ________

Service

☐ Jurat ☐ Acknowledgement

☐ Certification ☐ Oath/Affirmation

☐ Others ____________________

Document Type: ____________________

Driver's License : _____ /_____ /_____

☐ Individual

☐ Credible Witness

Thumb Print:

☐ Driver's License

☐ Passport

☐ Known Personally

☐ ID Card

☐ Other ________

ID#: ________

Issued By: ________

Issued On: __/__/__

Expired On: __/__/__

Individual

Name:
(print)

Address:

Phone:
(or email)

Signature:

Witness

Name:
(print)

Address:

Phone:
(or email)

Signature:

Notes

Notary Public Logbook Entry #83

Date & Time: ___/___/___ ___:___ am/pm

Place:

Fee: $ ___________

Travel: ___________

Service

- [ ] Jurat
- [ ] Acknowledgement
- [ ] Certification
- [ ] Oath/Affirmation
- [ ] Others ___________________________

Document Type: ___________________________

Driver's License : _____ /_____ /_____

- [ ] Individual
- [ ] Credible Witness

Thumb Print:

- [ ] Driver's License
- [ ] Passport
- [ ] Known Personally
- [ ] ID Card
- [ ] Other ___________

ID#: ___________

Issued By: ___________

Issued On: __/__/__

Expired On: __/__/__

Individual

Name:
(print)

Address:

Phone:
(or email)

Signature:

Witness

Name:
(print)

Address:

Phone:
(or email)

Signature:

Notes

Notary Public Logbook Entry #84

Date & Time: __/__/__ __:__ am/pm

Place:

Fee: $ ________

Travel: ________

Service

☐ Jurat ☐ Acknowledgement

☐ Certification ☐ Oath/Affirmation

☐ Others ____________

Document Type: ____________

Driver's License : _____ /_____ /_____

☐ Individual

☐ Credible Witness

Thumb Print:

☐ Driver's License

☐ Passport

☐ Known Personally

☐ ID Card

☐ Other ________

ID#: ________

Issued By: ________

Issued On: __/__/__

Expired On: __/__/__

Individual

Name:
(print)

Address:

Phone:
(or email)

Signature:

Witness

Name:
(print)

Address:

Phone:
(or email)

Signature:

Notes

Notary Public Logbook Entry #85

Date & Time: __/__/__ __:__ am/pm

Place:

Fee: $ ________

Travel: ________

Service

☐ Jurat ☐ Acknowledgement

☐ Certification ☐ Oath/Affirmation

☐ Others ____________

Document Type: ____________

Driver's License : ____ /____ /____

☐ Individual

☐ Credible Witness

Thumb Print:

☐ Driver's License

☐ Passport

☐ Known Personally

☐ ID Card

☐ Other ________

ID#: ________

Issued By: ________

Issued On: __/__/__

Expired On: __/__/__

Individual

Name:
(print)

Address:

Phone:
(or email)

Signature:

Witness

Name:
(print)

Address:

Phone:
(or email)

Signature:

Notes

Notary Public Logbook Entry #86

Date & Time: __/__/__ __:__ am/pm

Place:

Fee: $ ________

Travel: ________

Service

- [ ] Jurat
- [ ] Acknowledgement
- [ ] Certification
- [ ] Oath/Affirmation
- [ ] Others ________________

Document Type: ________________

Driver's License : _____ /_____ /_____

- [ ] Individual
- [ ] Credible Witness

Thumb Print:

- [ ] Driver's License
- [ ] Passport
- [ ] Known Personally
- [ ] ID Card
- [ ] Other ________

ID#: ________

Issued By: ________

Issued On: __/__/__

Expired On: __/__/__

Individual

Name:
(print)

Address:

Phone:
(or email)

Signature:

Witness

Name:
(print)

Address:

Phone:
(or email)

Signature:

Notes

Notary Public Logbook Entry #87

Date & Time: __/__/__ __:__ am/pm

Place:

Fee: $ ________

Travel: ________

Service

- [ ] Jurat
- [ ] Acknowledgement
- [ ] Certification
- [ ] Oath/Affirmation
- [ ] Others ________________

Document Type: ________________

Driver's License : _____ /_____ /_____

- [ ] Individual
- [ ] Credible Witness

Thumb Print:

- [ ] Driver's License
- [ ] Passport
- [ ] Known Personally
- [ ] ID Card
- [ ] Other ________

ID#: ________

Issued By: ________

Issued On: __/__/__

Expired On: __/__/__

Individual

Name:
(print)

Address:

Phone:
(or email)

Signature:

Witness

Name:
(print)

Address:

Phone:
(or email)

Signature:

Notes

Notary Public Logbook Entry #88

Date & Time: __/__/__ __:__ am/pm

Place:

Fee: $ ________

Travel: ________

Service

☐ Jurat ☐ Acknowledgement

☐ Certification ☐ Oath/Affirmation

☐ Others ____________

Document Type: ____________

Driver's License : ____ /____ /____

☐ Individual

☐ Credible Witness

Thumb Print:

☐ Driver's License

☐ Passport

☐ Known Personally

☐ ID Card

☐ Other ________

ID#: ________

Issued By: ________

Issued On: __/__/__

Expired On: __/__/__

Individual

Name:
(print)

Address:

Phone:
(or email)

Signature:

Witness

Name:
(print)

Address:

Phone:
(or email)

Signature:

Notes

Notary Public Logbook Entry #89

Date & Time: __/__/__ __:__ am/pm

Place:

Fee: $ ________

Travel: ________

Service

☐ Jurat ☐ Acknowledgement

☐ Certification ☐ Oath/Affirmation

☐ Others ____________

Document Type: ____________

Driver's License : ____ /____ /____

☐ Individual

☐ Credible Witness

Thumb Print:

☐ Driver's License

☐ Passport

☐ Known Personally

☐ ID Card

☐ Other ________

ID#: ________

Issued By: ________

Issued On: __/__/__

Expired On: __/__/__

Individual

Name:
(print)

Address:

Phone:
(or email)

Signature:

Witness

Name:
(print)

Address:

Phone:
(or email)

Signature:

Notes

Notary Public Logbook Entry #90

Date & Time: __/__/__ __:__ am/pm

Place:

Fee: $ ________

Travel: ________

Service

☐ Jurat ☐ Acknowledgement

☐ Certification ☐ Oath/Affirmation

☐ Others ____________

Document Type: ____________

Driver's License : _____ /_____ /_____

☐ Individual

☐ Credible Witness

Thumb Print:

☐ Driver's License

☐ Passport

☐ Known Personally

☐ ID Card

☐ Other ________

ID#: ________

Issued By: ________

Issued On: __/__/__

Expired On: __/__/__

Individual

Name:
(print)

Address:

Phone:
(or email)

Signature:

Witness

Name:
(print)

Address:

Phone:
(or email)

Signature:

Notes

Notary Public Logbook Entry #91

Date & Time: __/__/__ __:__ am/pm

Place:

Fee: $ ________

Travel: ________

Service

- [ ] Jurat
- [ ] Acknowledgement
- [ ] Certification
- [ ] Oath/Affirmation
- [ ] Others ________________

Document Type: ________________

Driver's License : _____ /_____ /_____

- [ ] Individual
- [ ] Credible Witness

Thumb Print:

- [ ] Driver's License
- [ ] Passport
- [ ] Known Personally
- [ ] ID Card
- [ ] Other ________

ID#: ________

Issued By: ________

Issued On: __/__/__

Expired On: __/__/__

Individual

Name:
(print)

Address:

Phone:
(or email)

Signature:

Witness

Name:
(print)

Address:

Phone:
(or email)

Signature:

Notes

Notary Public Logbook Entry #92

Date & Time: __/__/__ __:__ am/pm

Place:

Fee: $ ________

Travel: ________

Service

☐ Jurat ☐ Acknowledgement

☐ Certification ☐ Oath/Affirmation

☐ Others ____________

Document Type: ____________

Driver's License : ____ /____ /____

☐ Individual

☐ Credible Witness

Thumb Print:

☐ Driver's License

☐ Passport

☐ Known Personally

☐ ID Card

☐ Other ________

ID#: ________

Issued By: ________

Issued On: __/__/__

Expired On: __/__/__

Individual

Name:
(print)

Address:

Phone:
(or email)

Signature:

Witness

Name:
(print)

Address:

Phone:
(or email)

Signature:

Notes

Notary Public Logbook Entry #93

Date & Time: __/__/__ __:__ am/pm

Place:

Fee: $ ________

Travel: ________

Service

☐ Jurat ☐ Acknowledgement

☐ Certification ☐ Oath/Affirmation

☐ Others ____________________

Document Type: ____________________

Driver's License : _____ /_____ /_____

☐ Individual

☐ Credible Witness

Thumb Print:

☐ Driver's License

☐ Passport

☐ Known Personally

☐ ID Card

☐ Other ________

ID#: ________

Issued By: ________

Issued On: __/__/__

Expired On:__/__/__

Individual

Name:
(print)

Address:

Phone:
(or email)

Signature:

Witness

Name:
(print)

Address:

Phone:
(or email)

Signature:

Notes

Notary Public Logbook Entry #94

Date & Time: __/__/__ __:__ am/pm

Place:

Fee: $ ________

Travel: ________

Service

- [ ] Jurat
- [ ] Acknowledgement
- [ ] Certification
- [ ] Oath/Affirmation
- [ ] Others ________

Document Type: ________

Driver's License : ____ /____ /____

- [ ] Individual
- [ ] Credible Witness

Thumb Print:

- [ ] Driver's License
- [ ] Passport
- [ ] Known Personally
- [ ] ID Card
- [ ] Other ________

ID#: ________

Issued By: ________

Issued On: __/__/__

Expired On: __/__/__

Individual

Name:
(print)

Address:

Phone:
(or email)

Signature:

Witness

Name:
(print)

Address:

Phone:
(or email)

Signature:

Notes

Notary Public Logbook Entry #95

Date & Time: __/__/__ __:__ am/pm

Place:

Fee: $ ________

Travel: ________

Service

- [ ] Jurat
- [ ] Acknowledgement
- [ ] Certification
- [ ] Oath/Affirmation
- [ ] Others ________________

Document Type: ________________

Driver's License : _____ /_____ /_____

- [ ] Individual
- [ ] Credible Witness

Thumb Print:

- [ ] Driver's License
- [ ] Passport
- [ ] Known Personally
- [ ] ID Card
- [ ] Other ________

ID#: ________

Issued By: ________

Issued On: __/__/__

Expired On: __/__/__

Individual

Name:
(print)

Address:

Phone:
(or email)

Signature:

Witness

Name:
(print)

Address:

Phone:
(or email)

Signature:

Notes

Notary Public Logbook Entry #96

Date & Time: __/__/__ __:__ am/pm

Place:

Fee: $ ______

Travel: ______

Service

☐ Jurat ☐ Acknowledgement

☐ Certification ☐ Oath/Affirmation

☐ Others __________

Document Type: __________

Driver's License : ____ /____ /____

☐ Individual

☐ Credible Witness

Thumb Print:

☐ Driver's License

☐ Passport

☐ Known Personally

☐ ID Card

☐ Other ______

ID#: ______

Issued By: ______

Issued On: __/__/__

Expired On: __/__/__

Individual

Name:
(print)

Address:

Phone:
(or email)

Signature:

Witness

Name:
(print)

Address:

Phone:
(or email)

Signature:

Notes

Notary Public Logbook Entry #97

Date & Time: __/__/__ __:__ am/pm

Place:

Fee: $ ________

Travel: ________

Service

- [ ] Jurat
- [ ] Acknowledgement
- [ ] Certification
- [ ] Oath/Affirmation
- [ ] Others ________

Document Type: ________

Driver's License : ____ /____ /____

- [ ] Individual
- [ ] Credible Witness

Thumb Print:

- [ ] Driver's License
- [ ] Passport
- [ ] Known Personally
- [ ] ID Card
- [ ] Other ________

ID#: ________

Issued By: ________

Issued On: __/__/__

Expired On: __/__/__

Individual

Name:
(print)

Address:

Phone:
(or email)

Signature:

Witness

Name:
(print)

Address:

Phone:
(or email)

Signature:

Notes

Notary Public Logbook Entry #98

Date & Time: __/__/__ __:__ am/pm

Place:

Fee: $ ________

Travel: ________

Service

☐ Jurat ☐ Acknowledgement

☐ Certification ☐ Oath/Affirmation

☐ Others ____________

Document Type: ____________

Driver's License : ____ /____ /____

☐ Individual

☐ Credible Witness

Thumb Print:

☐ Driver's License

☐ Passport

☐ Known Personally

☐ ID Card

☐ Other ________

ID#: ________

Issued By: ________

Issued On: __/__/__

Expired On: __/__/__

Individual

Name:
(print)

Address:

Phone:
(or email)

Signature:

Witness

Name:
(print)

Address:

Phone:
(or email)

Signature:

Notes

Notary Public Logbook Entry #99

Date & Time: ___/___/___ ___:___ am/pm

Place:

Fee: $ ___________

Travel: ___________

Service

- [ ] Jurat
- [ ] Acknowledgement
- [ ] Certification
- [ ] Oath/Affirmation
- [ ] Others ______________________

Document Type: ______________________

Driver's License : _____ /_____ /_____

- [ ] Individual
- [ ] Credible Witness

Thumb Print:

- [ ] Driver's License
- [ ] Passport
- [ ] Known Personally
- [ ] ID Card
- [ ] Other ___________

ID#: ___________

Issued By: ___________

Issued On: __/__/__

Expired On: __/__/__

Individual

Name:
(print)

Address:

Phone:
(or email)

Signature:

Witness

Name:
(print)

Address:

Phone:
(or email)

Signature:

Notes

Notary Public Logbook Entry #100

Date & Time: __/__/__ __:__ am/pm

Place:

Fee: $ ______

Travel: ______

Service

- [ ] Jurat
- [ ] Acknowledgement
- [ ] Certification
- [ ] Oath/Affirmation
- [ ] Others ______

Document Type: ______

Driver's License : ___ /___ /___

- [ ] Individual
- [ ] Credible Witness

Thumb Print:

- [ ] Driver's License
- [ ] Passport
- [ ] Known Personally
- [ ] ID Card
- [ ] Other ______

ID#: ______

Issued By: ______

Issued On: __/__/__

Expired On: __/__/__

Individual

Name:
(print)

Address:

Phone:
(or email)

Signature:

Witness

Name:
(print)

Address:

Phone:
(or email)

Signature:

Notes

Made in United States
Troutdale, OR
11/03/2026

56844452R00118